PASS–ALONG

Promises

Inspiration for
WOMEN

Judy

© 2005 by Barbour Publishing, Inc.

ISBN 1-59310-639-4

interior images © Photonica

Published by Barbour Publishing, Inc., P.O. Box 719, Uhrichsville, Ohio 44683, www.barbourbooks.com

Our mission is to publish and distribute inspirational products offering exceptional value and biblical encouragement to the masses.

ecpa Member of the
Evangelical Christian
Publishers Association

Printed in China.
5 4 3 2

PASS-ALONG
Promises

Inspiration for
WOMEN

WRITTEN AND COMPILED BY
HOPE CLARKE

BARBOUR
PUBLISHING

TO SAMANTHA~

You are my shining star,
my bright light in the darkness.
No mother could have ever
asked for a more precious,
more beautiful daughter.
I love you with my whole heart.

*You are a
unique and
beautiful woman.*

"THE LORD DOES NOT LOOK AT

THE THINGS MAN LOOKS AT.

MAN LOOKS AT THE OUTWARD

APPEARANCE, BUT THE LORD

LOOKS AT THE HEART."

1 SAMUEL 16:7

*Laughter is
the sun that drives winter
from the human face.*

VICTOR HUGO

. . .

*R*EJOICE IN THE L<small>ORD</small> AND

BE GLAD, YOU RIGHTEOUS;

SING, ALL YOU WHO ARE

UPRIGHT IN HEART!

P<small>SALM</small> 32:11

*Your beauty shines
through when you are
true to yourself and
listen to your heart.*

. . .

$\mathcal{H}$E WHO HAS CLEAN HANDS AND A

PURE HEART, WHO DOES NOT LIFT

UP HIS SOUL TO AN IDOL OR

SWEAR BY WHAT IS FALSE.

HE WILL RECEIVE BLESSING FROM

THE LORD AND VINDICATION

FROM GOD HIS SAVIOR.

PSALM 24:4–5

*Optimism is
the faith that
leads to achievement.
Nothing can be done
without hope and confidence.*

HELEN KELLER

. . .

May the God of hope fill

you with all joy and peace

as you trust in him,

so that you may overflow

with hope by the power

of the Holy Spirit.

Romans 15:13

No matter what happens,
you have the power to
choose how to respond.

. . .

*T*hough the fig tree does not bud and there are no grapes on the vines, though the olive crop fails and the fields produce no food. . .yet I will rejoice in the Lord, I will be joyful in God my Savior.

Habakkuk 3:17–18

But all God's angels
come to us disguised. . . .

JAMES RUSSELL LOWELL

. . .

*F*OR HE WILL COMMAND HIS

ANGELS CONCERNING YOU TO

GUARD YOU IN ALL YOUR WAYS.

PSALM 91:11

God will protect you
and love you.
He will lift you
when you stumble.

. . .

If the Lord delights in a man's way, he makes his steps firm; though he stumble, he will not fall, for the Lord upholds him with his hand.

Psalm 37:23–24

*Indulge in
the peaceful silence
and contentment
you experience in
the Lord's presence.*

. . .

$\mathcal{A}$ND THE PEACE OF GOD,

WHICH TRANSCENDS ALL

UNDERSTANDING, WILL

GUARD YOUR HEARTS AND

YOUR MINDS IN CHRIST

JESUS.

PHILIPPIANS 4:7

You have many
beautiful gifts to
offer the world.
Give them freely
and with great love.

. . .

$\mathcal{D}$O NOT FORGET TO DO GOOD

AND TO SHARE WITH OTHERS,

FOR WITH SUCH SACRIFICES

GOD IS PLEASED.

HEBREWS 13:16

What lies behind us
and what lies before us
are tiny matters compared to
what lies within us.

RALPH WALDO EMERSON

"*B*Y THEIR FRUIT YOU WILL

RECOGNIZE THEM."

MATTHEW 7:16

There is in every
true woman's heart a
spark of heavenly fire,
which lies dormant in the
broad daylight of prosperity,
but which kindles up and
beams and blazes in the
dark hour of adversity.

WASHINGTON IRVING

$\mathcal{Y}$OU NEED TO PERSEVERE SO THAT

WHEN YOU HAVE DONE THE WILL

OF GOD, YOU WILL RECEIVE

WHAT HE HAS PROMISED.

HEBREWS 10:36

Trust God to
provide you with
the right words.

. . .

A WORD APTLY SPOKEN IS LIKE

APPLES OF GOLD IN SETTINGS

OF SILVER.

PROVERBS 25:11

Some people
come into our lives,
leave footprints on our hearts,
and we are never the same.

UNKNOWN

. . .

"As the Father has loved me,

so have I loved you."

John 15:9

The Lord has
richly blessed you!
. . .

Always giving thanks to God

the Father for everything,

in the name of our Lord

Jesus Christ.

Ephesians 5:20

*Your inner beauty
shines like the
most precious of jewels.*

. . .

A WIFE OF NOBLE CHARACTER

WHO CAN FIND?

SHE IS WORTH FAR MORE

THAN RUBIES.

PROVERBS 31:10

Celebrate each new day
in your life. . . .
Imagine the possibilities!

"*All* things are possible

with God."

Mark 10:27

*You will find as you
look back upon your life
that the moments when
you have truly lived are
the moments when you have
done things in the spirit of love.*

HENRY DRUMMOND

[*Love*] ALWAYS PROTECTS, ALWAYS

TRUSTS, ALWAYS HOPES, ALWAYS

PERSEVERES.

1 CORINTHIANS 13:7

Happiness is as a butterfly,
which, when pursued,
is always beyond our grasp,
but which,
if you will sit down quietly,
may alight upon you.

NATHANIEL HAWTHORNE

• • •

Rejoice in the Lord always.

I will say it again: Rejoice!

Philippians 4:4

You have
many talents to offer—
gifts from a
loving and generous God.

. . .

*T*HERE ARE DIFFERENT KINDS OF

GIFTS, BUT THE SAME SPIRIT.

THERE ARE DIFFERENT KINDS OF

SERVICE, BUT THE SAME LORD.

THERE ARE DIFFERENT KINDS OF

WORKING, BUT THE SAME GOD

WORKS ALL OF THEM IN ALL MEN.

1 CORINTHIANS 12:4–6

Hope, like faith,
is nothing if
it is not courageous.

THORNTON WILDER

. . .

We wait in hope for the

Lord; he is our help

and our shield.

Psalm 33:20

The future is
as bright as
the promises of God.

WILLIAM CAREY

I WILL INSTRUCT YOU AND TEACH

YOU IN THE WAY YOU SHOULD

GO; I WILL COUNSEL YOU

AND WATCH OVER YOU.

PSALM 32:8

Kick back,
and rejoice in
life's simple pleasures.

. . .

"Anyone who will not

receive the kingdom of

God like a little child

will never enter it."

Luke 18:17

*Faith expects from God
what is beyond
all expectation.*

ANDREW MURRAY

· · ·

"*I*F YOU BELIEVE, YOU WILL

RECEIVE WHATEVER YOU ASK

FOR IN PRAYER."

MATTHEW 21:22

Remember how much
you are loved.

. . .

"For God so loved the world that he gave his one and only Son, that whoever believes in him shall not perish but have eternal life."

John 3:16

Take one cup of cheer,
and call me in the morning!

· · ·

A CHEERFUL HEART IS GOOD

MEDICINE.

PROVERBS 17:22

Embrace the
wonder and excitement
each new day brings.

. . .

THE LORD GIVES STRENGTH TO HIS

PEOPLE; THE LORD BLESSES HIS

PEOPLE WITH PEACE.

PSALM 29:11

When life's burdens are
too heavy to bear,
the Lord will lift
your weary soul.

. . .

"*C*OME TO ME, ALL YOU WHO ARE

WEARY AND BURDENED, AND I

WILL GIVE YOU REST."

Matthew 11:28

Cast your worries
to the wind.
The heavenly Father
watches over you.

. . .

"Who of you by worrying

can add a single hour

to his life?"

Matthew 6:27

Be assured that
God will hear you.

. . .

"Ask and it will be given to you; seek and you will find; knock and the door will be opened to you."

Matthew 7:7

*Never be afraid
to trust an unknown future
to a known God.*

CORRIE TEN BOOM

. . .

COMMIT TO THE LORD WHATEVER

YOU DO, AND YOUR PLANS WILL

SUCCEED.

PROVERBS 16:3

Be the living expression
of God's kindness:
kindness in your face,
kindness in your eyes,
kindness in your smile.

MOTHER TERESA

Let us not become weary in doing good, for at the proper time we will reap a harvest if we do not give up. Therefore, as we have opportunity, let us do good to all people.

Galatians 6:9–10

You are a beacon to
those who surround you,
a light glowing in the darkness.

. . .

"No one lights a lamp and hides it in a jar or puts it under a bed. Instead, he puts it on a stand, so that those who come in can see the light."

Luke 8:16

You will be victorious
in your trials.

. . .

BLESSED IS THE MAN WHO

PERSEVERES UNDER TRIAL,

BECAUSE WHEN HE HAS STOOD

THE TEST, HE WILL RECEIVE

THE CROWN OF LIFE THAT

GOD HAS PROMISED TO

THOSE WHO LOVE HIM.

JAMES 1:12

Your life has been
a shining example to others.

. . .

REMIND THE PEOPLE TO BE SUBJECT TO RULERS AND AUTHORITIES, TO BE OBEDIENT, TO BE READY TO DO WHATEVER IS GOOD, TO SLANDER NO ONE, TO BE PEACEABLE AND CONSIDERATE, AND TO SHOW TRUE HUMILITY TOWARD ALL MEN.

TITUS 3:1–2

Weave in faith,
and God will find the thread.

PROVERB

. . .

"I TELL YOU THE TRUTH, IF YOU HAVE FAITH AS SMALL AS A MUSTARD SEED, YOU CAN SAY TO THIS MOUNTAIN, 'MOVE FROM HERE TO THERE' AND IT WILL MOVE. NOTHING WILL BE IMPOSSIBLE FOR YOU."

MATTHEW 17:20–21

You have a generous
and forgiving spirit.
. . .

"And when you stand praying, if you hold anything against anyone, forgive him, so that your Father in heaven may forgive you your sins."

MARK 11:25

*Your spirit lights
the way for
everyone around you.*

"LET YOUR LIGHT SHINE BEFORE

MEN, THAT THEY MAY SEE YOUR

GOOD DEEDS AND PRAISE YOUR

FATHER IN HEAVEN."

MATTHEW 5:16

*You are loved deeply
and unconditionally.*

. . .

This is how God showed his love among us: He sent his one and only Son into the world that we might live through him.

1 John 4:9

You are not alone
in your walk of faith.

. . .

$\mathcal{P}$URSUE RIGHTEOUSNESS, FAITH,

LOVE AND PEACE, ALONG WITH

THOSE WHO CALL ON THE LORD

OUT OF A PURE HEART.

2 TIMOTHY 2:22

A life with Christ
is a life of strength.

. . .

So then, just as you received Christ Jesus as Lord, continue to live in him, rooted and built up in him, strengthened in the faith as you were taught, and overflowing with thankfulness.

Colossians 2:6–7

Faith sees the invisible,
believes the unbelievable,
and receives the impossible.

CORRIE TEN BOOM

• • •

$\mathcal{N}$OW FAITH IS BEING SURE OF

WHAT WE HOPE FOR AND

CERTAIN OF WHAT WE DO

NOT SEE.

HEBREWS 11:1

When you walk in love,
you walk with God.

. . .

*A*S YOU HAVE HEARD FROM THE

BEGINNING, HIS COMMAND IS

THAT YOU WALK IN LOVE.

2 JOHN 6

As you have
carefully tended the garden
of your life with love,
peace, and understanding,
you have been an
inspiration to others.

. . .

$\mathcal{P}$EACEMAKERS WHO SOW IN

PEACE RAISE A HARVEST OF

RIGHTEOUSNESS.

JAMES 3:18

*The Lord is
your shield through
all of life's battles.*

PUT ON THE FULL ARMOR OF GOD,

SO THAT WHEN THE DAY OF EVIL

COMES, YOU MAY BE ABLE TO STAND

YOUR GROUND.

EPHESIANS 6:13

*The journey
may be difficult,
but your rewards
will be great.*

· · ·

"*E*NTER THROUGH THE NARROW GATE. FOR WIDE IS THE GATE AND BROAD IS THE ROAD THAT LEADS TO DESTRUCTION, AND MANY ENTER THROUGH IT. BUT SMALL IS THE GATE AND NARROW THE ROAD THAT LEADS TO LIFE, AND ONLY A FEW FIND IT."

MATTHEW 7:13–14